WHAT BRINGS YOU TO DEL AMO

Other Volumes in the Series

The Morse Poetry Prize EDITED BY GUY ROTELLA

WHAT BRINGS YOU TO DEL AMO

Virginia Chase Sutton

THE 2007 MORSE POETRY PRIZE

Selected and Introduced by Charles Harper Webb

Northeastern University Press
BOSTON

PUBLISHED BY UNIVERSITY PRESS OF NEW ENGLAND
HANOVER AND LONDON

Northeastern University Press
Published by University Press of New England,
One Court Street, Lebanon, NH 03766
www.upne.com
© 2007 by Virginia Chase Sutton
Printed in the United States of America
5 4 3 2 1

Library of Congress Cataloging-in-Publication Data can be found on the last page of the book.

Reprinted from *Cold Pluto:* "Yonder" by permission of Carnegie Mellon University Press © 1996 by Mary Ruefle.

Excerpt from "Diving into the Wreck" Copyright © 2002 by Adrienne Rich. Copyright © 1973 by W. W. Norton & Company, Inc., from THE FACT OF A DOORFRAME: SELECTED POEMS 1950–2001 by Adrienne Rich. Used by permission of the author and W. W. Norton & Company.

Excerpt from "The Shoes of Wandering" from THE BOOK OF NIGHTMARES by Galway Kinnell. Copyright © 1971, renewed 1998 by Galway Kinnell. Reprinted by permission of Houghton Mifflin Company. All rights reserved.

Excerpt from "Notes Composed in a Heat Wave" from *Blue on Blue Ground,* by Aaron Smith, © 2005. Reprinted by permission of the University of Pittsburgh Press.

"Housekeeping": Reprinted with permission from *Sweeping Beauty* edited by Pam Gemin, published by the University of Iowa Press.

"The Hypnotist" ["The Ecstatic Rapture"]: From *Fever Dreams,* edited by Leilani Wright and James Cervantes. © 1997 Leilani Wright and James Cervantes. Reprinted by permission of the University of Arizona Press.

"Drunk": Copyright © 2000 by the Antioch Review, Inc. First appeared in the *Antioch Review,* Vol. 58, No. 4. Reprinted by permission of the Editors. Reprinted with permission from *Are You Experienced* edited by Pam Gemin, published by the University of Iowa Press.

for John

But first you must be the sea
and swallow everything in your path.
    —Mary Ruefle

I came to explore the wreck.
The words are purposes.
The words are maps.
I came to see the damage that was done
and the treasures that prevail.

 —Adrienne Rich

On this road
on which I do not know how to ask for bread
on which I do not know how to ask for water,
this path
inventing itself
through jungles of burnt flesh, ground of ground
bones, crossing itself
at the odor of blood, and stumbling on . . .

 —Galway Kinnell

My doctor prescribes another pill.
So much work to feel
happy. I tell him I cried

this morning because we die,
because we are given back.

 —Aaron Smith

Contents

Acknowledgments

Grateful acknowledgment is made to the editors of the following publications where these poems, some of them since revised, first appeared, or are forthcoming:

Alimentum: "High Tea," "Life's a Banquet"

Antioch Review: "Drunk"

Coe Review: "What Brings You to Del Amo"

The MacGuffin: "Manic"

National Forum: "Bleeding Out," "The Afternoon My Mother Wears a Pillowcase Over Her Head"

Paris Review: "At the Barry M. Goldwater Gunnery Range"

Paterson Literary Review: "Ars Poetica"

Ploughshares: "The Tenants"

Quarterly West: "Nothing Ordinary," "The Ecstatic Rapture"

Western Humanities Review: "My Daughter Notices the Stranger"

Witness: "Loving the Juggler," "Twenty-Five Years a Headliner," "Water Landing"

"Ars Poetica" won first place in the Allen Ginsberg Poetry Award competition.

"Drunk" is anthologized in *Are You Experienced?* (University of Iowa Press, 2005).

"Housekeeping" is anthologized in *All This Useless Beauty: Contemporary Women Poets On Housework* (University of Iowa Press, 2005).

"The Ecstatic Rapture," titled "The Hypnotist," is anthologized in *Fever Dreams:Contemporary Arizona Poetry* (University of Arizona Press, 1997).

"The Tenants" is anthologized in *Turning Up the Leaves* (Coe College Press, 2000).

"St. Luke's Hospital" was finalist for the National Poetry Competition of the National Writers Union, judged by Adrienne Rich.

"Loving the Juggler" was commissioned by the Scottsdale Cultural Council, Scottsdale, Arizona, as part of a series on art and writing.

"Ars Poetica," "Last Day in Paris," and "How He Saves Me," appear in the chapbook titled *April: Poetry Anthology* (City of Tempe, Arizona, 2003).

"An Iowa Pork Princess Remembers" won first prize in the Tucson International Poetry Festival XV.

With deep thanks to many friends for their wisdom and support: Mark Doty, Michael Carter, Cynthia Schwartzberg Edlow, Aaron Smith, Philip Mandel, Josie Kearns, Roger Weingarten, Jimmy Berlin, and Catherine Hammond.

Profound thanks to Bruce Weigl who took on my poems and shaped them into a manuscript.

Thanks to Dr. Colin Ross and his program at Del Amo Hospital, where I was assisted in discovery and recovery. Thanks, too, to the therapists and other professionals there for their help.

Special thanks to the women I met in the hospital. Their identities are disguised here, but they are the bravest souls I've known. With brilliance and kindness, they shared their lives in the midst of terrible pain, cared about me, and listened to and believed in my work.

Thanks, too, to Thomas Gazda, M.D., for being the Muse, and for leading me through the terrain of the inner life in a world with little room for fascination and obsession.

And thanks to David Smart, M.A.; forever steadfast in the trenches, he rescued me and taught me the beauty and necessity of trust and grace.

Thanks also to H. J. Schulte, M.D., whose astute observations and constant vigilance have illuminated a path forward.

And thanks as well to the Ragdale Foundation, for residencies where many of these poems were written; to the Arizona Commission on the Arts, for financial support of work on this book; and to Vermont College's Post-Grad Summer Conference, for scholarship and support.

Introduction

The link between poetry and mental illness was recognized well before the time of Aristotle, who believed that poets and other creative persons tended toward "melancholia." Several studies have shown that writers are more likely than other artists to be depressed, and that poets are more likely to be depressed than fiction writers.[1] In a study published in 2001, the psychologist James Kaufman found what he termed "the Sylvia Plath effect": that female poets are more likely even than male poets to have been hospitalized or attempted suicide. In addition, the startling mental leaps and free associations of first-rate poets—their ability to access what Freud called the "primary process"—have much in common with the thoughts and perceptions associated with some kinds of mental illness.

In Virginia Chase Sutton's *What Brings You to Del Amo*, both poetry-and-mental-illness links are on display. Sutton's poems—many set in mental hospitals and/or dealing with psychiatric problems—delight with their fresh imagery, vivid perceptions, unusual perspectives, and general liveliness, even when their subject is suffering. They also explore less frequently chronicled aspects of mental illness, including the comedy, sexual highs/lows, and manic elation—*"this glory"*—of their bipolar narrator's life.

> *It's as fast as chugging boilermakers at Joe's bar*
> *or preening in a rummage sale rayon forties dress*
>
> *printed in phony pink Japanese symbols. Sometimes*
> *it's snatching plastic daffodils from someone's*
>
> *yard, convinced they're real or stealing*
> *a gold lamé sandal at a bar, leaving its owner*
>
> *to hobble home . . .*
>
> *. . . Or you*

---

1. The struggles with mental illness of Anne Sexton, Sylvia Plath, John Berryman, Delmore Schwartz, et al. are well known.

have sex with a guy you just met at Kentucky
Fried Chicken or you down more than one bottle of pink champagne

at midnight, then hitch to the 7-Eleven at noon to buy
a twelve-pack of beer . . .

"Copper Stars" details the narrator's trip to a tattoo parlor where she succeeds, at least temporarily, in joining her body, and by extension her life, to the beauty and magnificence of "a tangle of stars." "How He Saves Me" concerns a therapist helping the narrator to thwart her own suicidal impulses. "The Afternoon My Mother Wears a Pillowcase Over Her Head" is a bizarre, tragi-comic, and ultimately touching portrait of the narrator's elderly mother—not a well woman herself.

. . . Mother's sitting
in the green recliner, a cigarette
burning down to ash in her good right hand.
. . .

My mother's cut holes in the case but they don't
match her eyes.   How did she light
that cigarette? . . .

But *What Brings You to Del Amo* did not win the Morse Prize for its subject matter, fascinating as that is. This book pulses with vivid language and high energy. Some characters may be depressed, but the book is not depressing. Unlike those all-too-common collections that, like the poems inside, feel static, turgid, hard to move through, like rowing in mud, *What Brings You to Del Amo* pulls the reader along. The best of these poems come equipped with inboard motors, or slide into powerful currents that carry the reader with them, briskly and pleasurably, if not always comfortably. This book, in other words, is—to use a term not often applied to poetry—a *good read*.

Writing about mental illness can be an orgy of "Poor me, heroic me, crazy me, suffering me, misunderstood me, unique me, pathetic me, brilliant me, saintly me"—self-serving, sentimental, dull. Sutton dodges these poetry-sinking reefs and snags, avoiding self-pity and self-dramatization, at the same time grabbing the reader's attention and holding on. While other books by Baby Boomers tell and re-tell the by-now predictable struggle to come to terms with past glories and present lives, this one dives unabashedly into areas usually hidden, glossed over, hushed up.

In "High Tea," we're let in on "the family secret":

> . . . Eleanor wears a beret,
> holds the thin saucer and bone china cup
> while Great-aunt Mary Ellen, writer, beloved
> teacher, English professor, directs
> a pale stream into the delicate shell.
> . . .
>
> *The women are lovers,*
> my mother must whisper, loving
> this unfolding.

In "Thanksgiving," we learn about hospital food—"One slice of white meat's my request / in the cafeteria line, but it's all / the same, white and dark / compressed into a jellied loaf. . . . "—and how the narrator, at thirteen, prepared her own first turkey.

> I named the bird Fred, bathed
> his nakedness in the sink,
> closing my eyes to the bloody neck
> and packet of guts tucked inside.
> A pink spill draining . . .

"It starts with his tongue," the narrator says in "Telling My Cousins About Sex."

> . . . *Open a window*
> *when you're done.* The youngest cousin, forever excluded,
> speaks from the corner, *Why ever for?* I answer the mirror

above the chest as it bends close to our tangle
of arms and legs. *You'll smell him for days,* I say.
And then *You'll like it, you really will.*

In another poem, the poet's mother smokes cigars and wants to become a man; then, years later, the narrator is kissed by a man who used to be a woman. This poem, called "Nothing Ordinary," aptly describes the book you now hold in your hand. You won't easily forget the characters and events described in *What Brings You to Del Amo*. To say that Sutton makes art out of adversity is true; all good books of poems do that. Still, I applaud the courage and the craft required to write this extraordinary collection. I recommend it to you heartily.

Charles Harper Webb

WHAT BRINGS YOU TO DEL AMO

MANIC

It's as fast as chugging boilermakers at Joe's bar
or preening in a rummage sale rayon forties dress

printed in phony pink Japanese symbols. Sometimes
it's snatching plastic daffodils from someone's

yard, convinced they're real or stealing
a gold lamé sandal at a bar, leaving its owner

to hobble home. How about painting your parents'
basement in broad red, white and blue stripes,

then bored, quitting halfway through? It's
guzzling a fifth of whiskey on a dare and sending

a two-pound Candygram to a pal, billing it to a name
in the phonebook and deciding to rearrange

all the furniture at two a.m. and eating not one but
two hash brownies just to see what happens. It could be

drunkenly running on a rainy street, falling
and crawling the rest of the way home. Or you

have sex with a guy you just met at Kentucky
Fried Chicken or you down more than one bottle of pink champagne

at midnight, then hitch to the 7-Eleven at noon to buy
a twelve-pack of beer. Maybe you're half-naked, getting

tattooed on your right breast at Lake Geneva, Wisconsin,
the bikers cheering you on. Perhaps you've been up all night again,

reading the entire book because you can't wait or you're down at that dive
on the railroad tracks where you swallow quarter glasses

of Grain Belt, singing along to thirty-year-old jukebox songs
or maybe you just feel something rushing between your fingers,

gold rising into your mouth and head, knowing
you can do nothing to stop this glory, nothing.

HOUSEKEEPING

was never discussed, just frozen dinners occasionally
baked to the tiny iced heart in throw-away tin containers

or pork chops, raw and reckless in the pan
in the silent kitchen or dusty under the living room

couch. My mother's not domestic. Endless
Sunday afternoons she's visiting from the hospital.

After last fall's stroke, bedridden,
trying to walk, to hold her head still

on her neck. A red plaid cookbook's
teaching me to make pot roast, directions

like the buttery taste of meat too long
in the oven. My father wants me at the hospital,

helping with her wig as it falls goofy over her forehead,
missing the long loopy scar. *Can't,* I tell him,

this roast has to go in right now. What do we
know of multi-hued vegetables, how to tuck shiny

pieces beside the magenta meat? How
can we learn to live with her again,

silent conversations drowsy,
her metal bedpan neat in a paper sack? It's

easier to learn to cook, measuring
what's required, following directions

to the correct platter and spoon. The table's set
with plastic dishes, dark sunbursts

flat as our dinnertime faces. These stiff people
eat plain meat and ordinary vegetables,

my disappointment of a dull Midwestern language.
I'll do dishes, I call, avoiding the return

trip. Last year, my home economics teacher
taught the eighth grade girls

that unspotted glassware equals domestic contentment.
You've got the knack, she said one afternoon,

my little make believe kitchen
a gallery of pure light and clean pots.

NOTHING ORDINARY

My mother said *Oh, I never wanted daughters.*
She was smoking a cigar
in the breezeway after school, the bright
glow burning under her nose.
She said *I've decided to become a man,*
then shook off the ashes with her

left hand. Years later, while standing in a friend's kitchen
complaining of the heat, a strange man raised a fistful
of my brown hair in his big hand. My skin
was water white, dripping little beads

into my collar. He exhaled carefully
across my neck, the silver bracelet on his left wrist
a cold jangle along my skin. Close enough
for the tip of his tongue to taste me,
and he watched me shudder, lean
into his careful darkness and pencil mustache.

Later, my friend said *Do you like him? He's
a woman, though his breasts are gone.*
All that shivering flesh removed and black dot
nipples stitched to his flat chest. *How do you
ever know?* What's it like to be a man,

to wear black and draw in fine lines
above the upper lip. A man stood beside me
and was steeped in my sweat and some terrible
longing. Could I have been remade,
turned into a boy long ago,
allowed the ashes from my mother's

tightly rolled stogie to smear into my eyes,
blurring my gender? *Girls are such*
trouble, she used to say. *They cry*
too much. I didn't cry then, not ever.
I won't be a boy, I told her.

And you can't be a man. The cigar
burned down another inch,
losing liquid and light. *Are you sure,* she asked,

the voice the same when the dark man said *I know*
what you're thinking. Then his face moved
a little closer, a little sweeter, one kiss
closer to my mouth.

ST. LUKE'S HOSPITAL

Outside it's over one hundred degrees
and inside the air conditioning hasn't worked
on the psych ward for five days.

We're in sweat up to our chins.
In the plain-as-milk dayroom, old magazines
someone's donated, overflow like end of summer

roses, drooping last minute petals
over a cast off table. A number of patients
need to shower. The summer I first

read Mishima, he was already dead,
suicide's beautiful gesture. Only once
have I seen the brief film

made from the story, the dress rehearsal
for his death. Shot in black and white,
he's the soldier, kneeling

before the unsheathed sword. Everything's
taken care of: he's made love to his wife,
bathed, now it's time

for that bleak gray shudder.
Were those tears in his eyes? He holds
electric perfection in one hand.

White cloth cinches the soldier's belly.
How he waited forever for this moment,
his splendid flesh gleaming! Ready

to go. That same summer
I loved a man whose stomach muscles
rippled through his thin t-shirt,

sharper than the ritual I watched
on the screen, or read in any Japanese novel.
This summer's lasting too long.

SNOW ANGEL

Sunday afternoon, January,
we're just getting out of bed,
when I say *Do me a favor.*
And you answer *What?* I tell you
Don't call or come to see me again.

That's it, the last of four months of fucking. See
something inside is pulsing, not your embrace
or the wetness between my legs, but some wild,
wicked drowning like it isn't going to stop. I run out
to the hard-blast sky and yell *I know, I know, I know.*

Breathing hard, I have to sit in a drift, thrust
my almost purple hands into the snow. That roar,
no way to explain, my body spilling liquid, the absolutely
insatiable know. It divides men into fuckable or non-fuckable,
though in an emergency, who knows? You knock me over,

our last fuck spinning my seventeen-year-old ass
into the cold. You are a man I never cared
to know. Hey, picture me there, the black and gray
winter sky splitting only for me. I am a crazy
snow angel, burn my image, dig it into the snow.

THE ECSTATIC RAPTURE

Here is the man in a plain suit,
his ordinary striped tie tucked
behind too narrow lapels. The woman
lets him in, the hypnotist, *La Cirella.*

Soggy splotches his shoes leave
on the beige rug don't really matter.
They sip cocktails, hers an ice fog
of gin, his heavy bourbon. He reaches

for the sweet cherry with two manicured fingers
deep along the cold glassy bottom. The girl
watches from the kitchen, pours
fine shards of ice into the bucket, refills the metal trays

with tap water. *He doesn't look much
like a hypnotist,* she thinks. Where are
the tricks? The spangled ponies jumping
from thin air, the puff of smoke, explosions

of amber stars across some vast stage?
The woman calls her daughter in, wants *La Cirella*
to carve hollows beneath that throat, narrow
the breasts already straining beneath

the sailor suit. The girl has gathered
sweet peas from the yard, put their stalks
in water glasses on each table in the living room.
She likes their silly heads bending for more water,

petals tipped in a dim blush of color. Delicate hands
reach for her, pale half moons rising on each finger,
and suddenly, she knows what he can see
behind brass military buttons and sailcloth, down to her

last bone and bruise. Underneath that pale blue suit
his body rises, and she sees him
sticky against her mother, and then between her own
fat thighs. When he tells them to fall back on the sofa,

to follow the simple glitter of his watch with their eyes,
they do as they are told. They go willingly.
Last night the woman sat on the nightclub's
small stage and let her red curls tumble

when her head fell flush to her chest. He must have told
the audience that she was an animal just before death,
a white chicken ahead of the falling axe. Then
her body moved in some kind of desperate longing,

struggling against the folds of her smoky dress.
Bending and bending, she lowered her head
and danced on wobbly legs. Later, she asked him home
for cocktails, longing to close her eyes again

to his voice, the spin of an object, the jewel just put away.
The chrome sky outside cracks and leaks
while he decides which animals they shall become.

WHAT BRINGS YOU TO DEL AMO

Saturday and Sunday afternoons
stutter past; patients spend a few hours
listening to someone's particular story.
What brings us to Del Amo. This empty room,
empty shelves. One by one, we must speak.

And our journey, what puts us in a locked
psych ward for weeks, well, it's not
as if anyone could save us.

> *What brings you to Del Amo?* Steven asks.

Steven's a part time therapist,
working weekends, dead end shifts
no one bids for. To keep busy,

he provides the basic question.
Distraction. No picking at angry
sores marching up an ankle,

or the crust beneath gauze bandages,
though Nancy rewraps better
than any aide. She was a nurse

before the alters. Now all those traumatized pieces,
other voices and splintered interior selves,
pester her twenty-four-seven.

> *Does someone want to answer the question?* Steven asks.

Steven's a model of patience
in khaki pants, muted golf shirt,

black marker in hand, poised
at the white board. Someone says:

> *My mother was a drunk. Started*
> *passing out when I was eight: bed,*
> *couch, bathroom and kitchen floors.*
> *Dark urine spoiled the cushions,*
> *lapped the linoleum. She was an island of flesh,*
> *dead center in a yellow lake.*

*

Steven stops the questions, model of concern.

    Who are you, Steven asks one of us.

The woman wraps a stuffed animal
in a Winnie the Pooh baby blanket
before she says *I'm Little Amy.* She's a different
personality, not who he needs her to be.

Red snout and black floppy ears, her toy's
a dog. *I need Elizabeth,* Steven says, caps
the marker. *She's not here,* Little Amy answers,
clutches the bundle high on her chest. Elizabeth's
somewhere deep inside, can't come out right now.

    I need an adult. This is no place for children, Steven says.

And Little Amy leaves the room.

*

    Begin where you want to begin, Steven says.

He doesn't mean it. We're so weary
of repetition: number of suicide attempts
(methods used), mental health disorders (name them),
depression (when did it begin?), anonymous
sex (did your actions put you in danger?), blackouts
and drugs (list addictions). Number of rapes,
molestations (include all touch).

Steven, how many kinds of abuse exist?

Our weekend afternoons catalogue lists, someone
please answer his persistent question,
What brings you here?

*

I can always tell when my roommate becomes Jeff,
different personality, male swagger, demands house cigarettes.
Never mind that Lucy doesn't smoke.

Chain-smoking in the courtyard, Jeff fiddles
with the padlocks. *It's easy to bust out,*
if I wanted to. I believe him. Yesterday

he burned Lucy's cheek with a butt,
then skipped out. She took his punishment.
When Jeff's out I refuse to sleep

in our room. Sarah helps me drag
my mattress down to the Quiet Room
where the light's left on all night.

Makes sleeping tough but it bores
Jeff. He doesn't want me either.
He prefers to sleep alone.

*

The adult Heidi says:

> *The middle school band director*
> *squeezed my breasts, forced me*
> *to lie to the principal.*
> *When I stepped hard on his foot*
> *he made me look at the bruise,*
> *said what will I tell my mother?*
> *See what you did?*

Sometimes Heidi becomes Secret. It's
in her voice, the way it swivels
from her body, the way she jitters

in her chair. So many children here. How
to manage disassociation? Right now,
some of us are in parts, pieces, alters,
those named and unknown. *The Fat*

Woman wants to kill me, Nancy says.
And I don't know why. We didn't
do anything to her. Lucy's Miranda now,

covering the walls with elaborate collages,
bits and pieces, pictures and words ripped
from years of *National Geographic,*

the only magazine here. One
Sunday morning she shaped two figures
from a pile of coffee stirrers, the large plastic body

bending to hold the little one's hand.
The afternoon ends like all weekend afternoons.
Steven swipes the board, where one of our

histories, once under discussion, vanishes,
discarded, like an old library book. Hasn't been off
the shelf in years. You can see the fine

layer of dust and torn pages
mended by a steady hand.

DIET CLUB

On Saturday mornings, our neighbor,
Mrs. Benson, waits on her front porch. We hurry
to the blue and white bathroom,

the scale resting on the tile floor.
Never cheating, we don't ask one another
where the black line stops. Every week

I say *I haven't lost a pound.* She's majestic
on the fur-covered toilet lid, confiding diet tips
over the crash of her five kids against the door.

Leaving, I squirm past knowing eyes, the son
who sits behind me in sixth grade. No one ever
notices me. My mother's not a classroom helper,

doesn't know jack about PTA or Girl Scouts or even
Home Room Mom, yet this club is her idea. *Force
the weight off,* she explains, *before it's too late.*

Stomping in puddles, scraping the sidewalk,
I'm later each time until my mother says
I give up. But she doesn't. *Secret,* she whispers,

and pours a fistful of pills into my cupping hands.
Her cultivated taste for bourbon
and pills made her forget food long before.

They work. Sullen and wide-hipped, I swallow them.
My heart's hit dead-center. Heavy breath
on my face, her broken eyes don't notice

later, when my bottle's empty. I've thrown them away.
She thinks this is the trick, *I know it works,* she says.
This time she's sure.

ARS POETICA

She unfolds a bent staple the way
someone unwraps a creased handkerchief,
smoothing the edges open. Without
a mirror, she cuts into her face. The staple
scrapes from forehead into the crease

of her mouth. Deep red kisses
well along the ragged scratch.
Someone removes the cap
from a cheap pen, saws her left wrist
until it separates, bleeding. She spends

the night sitting in the hallway
outside my room. At midnight I crouch
beside her, whisper *Come back, come
back.* A pillow's untouched and someone's
left her a small stuffed dog. The famous

psychiatrist who runs this place challenges
me to write a poem, his face blooming
via video conference call all the way
from Dallas. *It can be,* he says,
about nothing. I'm already dead.

He tries to stump me with quotations
from Blake and Eliot. *Buddy,* I want
to tell him, *I'm medicated off my ass.*
Last count ten different pills, but I don't
self harm, so the staff opens a little office

and I'm left alone. Nearly three hours later,
I have a couple of lines. I wrap myself
in a blue hospital blanket, head to the dayroom

where everyone's watching TV. Someone
turns the volume down. *Did you write*

a poem? They want to hear it, my suicide
poem, but why tell them what they've
already lived? On the third evening here
my roommate unthreaded the string
from her sweatshirt's hood, wrapped it tight

around her neck. Not a hanging, exactly,
more like strangulation. It took two nurses
to unwind her. She was sent to another ward,
watched around the clock, dressed in a paper gown
and a paper blanket to keep her safe. And me,

left alone to write a poem after weeks
of observation? I sit in an office chair
and try to work, don't even check the clock.
Maybe I miss the mandatory fifteen minute
check-ins, click of the flashlight

in my face, fists banging on a closed
bathroom door, always someone
with a clipboard and careful little notes:
*Patient in the unused office for two hours
and forty-five minutes. She did not*

self harm. How odd to suddenly
be unwatched. When I read the poem
to my therapist, she sits for a minute,
says *Somehow I thought*
it would be much longer.

AT THE BARRY M. GOLDWATER GUNNERY RANGE

in Gila Bend, Arizona, all's gone still
with his death, the entire satellite base
draped in black garlands, even the old
soda machine outside the commissary. Someone's

wrapped bunting around two elderly airplanes,
display pieces that haven't been flown in twenty-five
years, military remnants that never rust
in endless desert. Just a few years ago

I drove eighty-five miles from Phoenix
twice a week to teach a composition class.
During breaks, soldiers gathered outside
in the heat, scanning the flat sky. Then one night

out in the hallway, a soldier tapped my chest,
said, *How I love you, can't you tell?* Gin fumes
drifted under my nose, a fever breaking. *Don't you see
that I'm too old for this,* he asked, then cried as MPs

dragged him into the dusty shadows, his feet
kicking up little sparks. *Don't forget me,* he called.
Back in the narrow classroom, one young man
explained, *As the highest ranking military person here,*

I offer apologies. The entire force is dishonored.
I've heard the Space Sky Motel in town offers
the Republican Special, two nights in the Barry M.
Goldwater suite for $29.95, plus continental breakfast.

Always I wanted to shout *My parents told me he was
the enemy* each time I pulled up to the guardhouse and

the soldier said, *Present ID and get out of the car.*
But I never said a word as the same tall man searched

my car, his flashlight's dull beam the only glimmering
light on the dirt road. I thought of all the patient
soldiers driving the flat sharp perimeters of the quiet
base, over and over, nothing to do but wait.

COPPER STARS

I want a tangle of stars, I tell her
and she draws a line on the fat pad
over my left shoulder, dissolving
down my back. *Honey,* she says, *I've tattooed
them from Portland, Oregon, to Portland, Maine.*

Driving down to Bisbee last year,
the closest I've come to Mexico,
desert hills and mountain edges
were purple smears over the hard smack
of highway. I headed into the corkscrew

of abandoned mining pits, shacks, the town
stacked inside an empty bowl.
How many steps through sulfur clouds,
the taint still as water inside a clawfoot tub?
Out on the verandah, the day finished,

a crocheted doily on the yellow afternoon.
I want the stars to open, I tell her, stars blown
inside out, the bite on my skin. Indigo outlines
like cheap ink. *Sure, sure,* she answers,
then *I'm adding little comets.*

It feels good. New explosions popping
over weepy blue threads. *Maybe a little lavender,
for color,* I say, recalling broken historic markers
and deserted shops back when copper went bust.
A thin shimmer, a tin roof grasping the last bit

of night sky before sunrise, old stone steps
forgotten in corners. The kind of light
that's down some mine shaft someone started digging

in the dark. Remember the sudden snow shower
in the desert, how white chilled the edges? *No problem,*

and she shifts her grip on my arm. All I want
is a little color to ignite this row of shabby stars,
moonstruck and loopy, like an old postmark
pressed across my smooth flesh.

THANKSGIVING

One slice of white meat's my request
in the cafeteria line but it's all
the same, white and dark
compressed into a jellied loaf. I take it
anyway. At thirteen I made
my first turkey, more than twenty pounds,
for three people. Mother was in a coma
after brain surgery, my father
so distracted, my sister locked in her room.
I named the bird Fred, bathed
his nakedness in the sink,
closing my eyes to the bloody neck
and packet of guts tucked inside.
A pink spill draining. I did it
all: potatoes, stuffing,
pumpkin pie out of the can. More
than thirty years later I'm at a hospital table
with seven patients, our meal
on heavy paper plates. We're allowed
one container of low-calorie
imitation cranberry sauce apiece.
It's only noon, so much time
before the day ends and we abandon
ourselves to meds and sleep. No seconds
allowed here. A patient suggests
we each speak of thankfulness.
My mind's an empty plate. Early evening,
a visitor brings Lucy an entire dinner
on a disposable plate wrapped in foil.
It's still warm. We all pull
chairs to the table, watch her eat
the plain, holiday food. Then a nurse
walks over, her pockets stuffed

with candy. She hands a bag
of chocolate to each one of us.
Because it's Thanksgiving,
she says, and we deserve a blessing.

HIGH TEA

—*Smith College, 1946*

Twin china pots on ecru crochet
differ only by a faded rosebud's
partial unfurling. This is the family secret
I've heard all my life: aging silver teaspoons
monogrammed with someone else's
initials, heavy cream perfect

in my great-aunt's cut glass pitcher.
My parents arrive for tea just days after
their elopement. Eleanor wears a beret,
holds the thin saucer and bone china cup
while Great-aunt Mary Ellen, writer, beloved
teacher, English professor, directs
a pale stream into the delicate shell.
It's *Royal Doulton,* the set safe now
in my china closet, patterned in lazy
fall gardens trellising up and over

each spout. *The women are lovers,*
my mother must whisper, loving
this unfolding. I can explain the rest
of the day by heart; how my father
begins to watch the lovers while he learns
the precise rehearsal of crystaled sugar,
the proper grasp of silver tongs. *Black currant,*

jasmine, oolong, he mouths the litany
of tea leaves. Trays of sandwiches spin
into pinwheels. How well Great-aunt Mary Ellen
knows the flowery taste of her lover's
mouth, the twist of her tongue sampling
each glowing bite. A Classics professor, Eleanor

recites in Latin, in Greek. Bishop's hats,
madeleines, strawberries in eddies
of chocolate. He can't decide so Eleanor
smiles at my mother, fills his plate
with shortbread and scones,
dips a well of clotted cream and cherry jam,

slides it to his astonished hands.
He must wonder at their bodies, lovers,
as my mother teases a candied violet
between his lips, savors the sweetness
gathering inside his mouth. *We name our daughters
for them*, my mother explains to her brand-new
country boy husband. This afternoon my parents
like the women, the tiny iced cakes, the tiered racks
of shiny tea things. I know my mother slides
her pretty tongue between his teeth.

LIFE'S A BANQUET

Most patients toss their entire meals into the garbage,
and who can blame us? Two doughy pancakes
or a box of *Cap'n Crunch*, sticky tofu stir fry, maybe
an over-cooked chicken breast. Still, it's better
than my mother's cooking or my own. I learn

an anorexic trick—carry a huge cup of diet soda
all day. A series of little sips. Kills the appetite.
Eating disorder patients slip across the hall
to purge in my bathroom because theirs is locked.
I smell sour leftovers though they flush and flush.

What's the best meal you ever had, a skinny patient asks.
I don't remember particulars though my purse rested
on a tapestry stool and the waiter poured from a plastic bottle
of *Evian.* For an entire week, the cafeteria gives me
a steamed turkey sandwich at lunch. No reason

for the yellow cheese sopping into the bread and the meat
floppy like a recently slaughtered carcass. The dietitian
has mean black eyes. We can't have peanut butter unless
it's breakfast, and never extra bread. We grow adept
at stealing. Once Nancy fingered six cookies

while Roxy coated the table with a thin layer of jelly.
Next meal she said *Someone better mop up this stickiness.*
We all laughed, our pockets bursting with hard boiled eggs,
sliced pickles, stuff from the salad bar, collecting
for a late night feast though most of it was destined
for the trash.

AN IOWA PORK PRINCESS REMEMBERS

My crown was a circlet of sparkle
and flame, uneasy atop the long slick
of my yellow hair. I wore it the week
of the State Fair in '74

when all the county princesses
held court in the agricultural building.
Dressed in white, we were a mirage of angels,
our bouquets of ivory glads leaking summer's
humidity from blunt cut stalks.

That was the first time I heard them. The piggy
voices were soprano, as sweet as a forkful
of their tender, shredded flesh. They said
We died for each of you, to make you queenly,

and their rich voices rose, frothing around us
like a huge lacy slip, a flurry of rice
on someone's wedding day. I still hear
their glorious chants *For you, for you,*
though I've nearly forgotten the trip to Des Moines,

posing on the courthouse steps in our seamless
formality. *We remember your happiness,*
your grace. And they do. They've gone
to canneries and packing plants
and still they cry *Pickled and succulent,*
in brine, we continue our song. They recall
the sweep of my gown, the summer I was royalty,
supreme in my ice tiara. Little skeletons,
sing. *No sacrifice too great.* Sing again.

We are sweet summer flowers. The pigs remember
the moment, my elbow length gloves, each
button and sliver of glitter. *We steam.*
They call me, knuckle and bone. *We steam.*

LOVING THE JUGGLER

Late at night when the narrow
wheels of the train are clacking,

and when my heart is beating
as if it will never stop, he calls

to me. *My dimpled dolly,* his arms
flung open, sweat tumbling

from oily leather hands. In the moment
he snakes around my hips, drooling

on my rippling thighs. *Oh, little
mountains,* he sings as the sheet slips,

bedclothes a pale knot, his taffeta costume
shooting stars, little pinpricks of light

all along my swells and curves. Sometimes
we feed the elephants after the last show,

let them nibble leftover peanuts from our palms
as we move in their slow cadence, stately

as their wrinkled skins, trunks reaching
blind towards the kind face next door.

Someone whispers *Jack* when he curls
my hair into tender sausages,

a tumble into my wide bodice, trickling
down the back of my satin gown,

an enormous sweep of blue, black
as any post-midnight sky. *What does he*

look like without makeup, a showgirl
wonders between acts. How they adore

the faithful slide of his shoes on sawdust,
the tricks as he capers around the ring, a blur

of stiff ruffles. And I love his pancake self,
whiteness smoothed across his face, frosting

the sharp wings of his neck and back.
Leave it on, I tell him when both hands hold

my breast to his puckering mouth.
In every town our stages sit side by side.

Wanda the Wondrous, my banner billowing
above the low couch, clutch of pillows and soft

velvet where I recline as the marks pause
before us. I'm watching Juggling Jack.

He reaches a long arm to unfasten the string of beads
from my throat, and in the big silence,

he unspools each bead in a jumble of heat, scrolling
the pieces over his slippery hands.

TWENTY-FIVE YEARS A HEADLINER

Face it, the old gal was born for the business. Sturdy legs,
acres of crinkly skin, her contortionist trunk fielding

baskets, bottles, a million other circus props. How many
showgirls climbed her dusty wide back, loving the gentle way

she rocked them around the ring? All those clowns dangling
from her jaws while she'd spin, rocketing dizzy circles.

And talented! Not every elephant can dance the two-step,
twirl fluorescent hoops, clang a tambourine, and shower

the first three rows with confetti blown from her trunk.
But lately, Flora's been dreamy. She doesn't care about horses

cantering alongside or even for the acrobat hanging
by her hair far above the ring. She's thinking of hay,

enough for forever, how it ripens just so beneath a hot
summer sky. And she imagines the world's largest Jacuzzi,

oh sinking all the way in, aching knees and spine blasted
in bone-melting water. Beloved Flora! So many assist

her retirement fund. At five bucks a pop they line up after
the show for a souvenir photo. Profile only, Flora insists,

one little eye gleaming. Her tired trunk's coiled like the old days.
Back when Flora trumpeted show time, entire body balancing

on one leg, giant mystery rising, a slamdance kid, ready.

TELLING MY COUSINS ABOUT SEX

Telling my cousins about sex
occupies an entire Christmas afternoon
upstairs on my great-grandmother's bed.
Below, thready hits from the forties spin off
the old piano, the muffled noise of Indiana
twangs. *It starts with his tongue,*
I tell the three sisters, and their narrow faces sharpen.
I explain too much: his body's shove deep
into the mattress, slick colors and skin tints,
our slow travel to the body's end. *Does*
it hurt, one asks, picking at her skirt's
gray pleats. Almost identical, these girls
with long hair dividing the centers of their high foreheads
and neat brows. So I sit up, whisper *Open a window*
when you're done. The youngest cousin, forever excluded,
speaks from the corner *Why ever for?* I answer the mirror
above the chest as it bends close to our tangle
of arms and legs. *You'll smell him for days,* I say.
And then *You'll like it, you really will.*
They lean on skinny necks as I describe
how my hands arrange his skin's burnt pleasures,
his cock, and the dark bruises of his body,
leave nothing unfinished.

AN OLD MAN'S ATONEMENT IN TRAUMA GROUP

Truth is a protector, Lucy tells us. *She's like a boil*
on your forehead growing bigger, taking everything
in. She guards the system, decides what we need,
then tells us.

> *I hate sleeping with my father, press of his legs*
> *against me. How I ride the bed's edge, hope*
> *his body won't press into mine.*

Someone's crying. She walks to the circle's center, pulls a wad
of tissue from the box where the therapist left it. The therapist insists
grief is not intrusive. The old man, perpetrator, startles, struggles
out of his chair, the door clicks. *Bastard,* I think. *Remember this*
when you're close to a little girl.

> *What happens in the bed I cannot remember.*
> *I offer him to my sister but she refuses.*

Many women are crying, this safe place where we voice
our stories, litter of pieces, share as much trauma as we dare.

> *There was something between us, always. And I knew it*
> *in his kiss, the way he captured my lips though I ducked,*
> *tried to hide from his gooey mouth.*

The therapist asks over the tears, all the noses blowing *How*
does it feel to say something so terrible?

The old man returns to Trauma Group. No longer triggered
by our truths. The old man will speak to an empty chair,
psych invention. All have the same frayed padding,
knotted blue cover, a bitch to get your ass out of after
you've been sitting for hours.

Pretend this empty chair is your wife. Imagine.
What do you need to say?

James answers *Beverly, I'm sorry for destroying our family, leaving you alone*
to face the town and friends. Now I'm morally clean. God has forgiven me.

The empty chair is motionless. The old man leans, one hand
brushes the air.

I've done everything required. Jail, this hospital program. God hears
my wholesome prayers.

We witness his atonement. But better disassociation, vanish
from this stuffy room into the California sun outside. My slipper stubs
the carpet. I want to slap him with my bare open hand, knock
his false teeth from his jaw. Let's see some real tears. Steady breath:
in and out, almost too much trouble.

Are you ready for a little feedback? The therapist asks flatly.

And their voices splinter: *maybe she'll forgive ... your daughters,*
granddaughters ... I cried for you, James.

I don't believe. Just another wall of words.

Dues paid, how very biblical. Yellow face quivering, silky mustache floats
above your upper lip, you're any old man. Three granddaughters
you hurt with hands clasped in your lap, fingers still.

We're always indoors, either this room or that. Small airplanes
drone overhead, careful spins before heading to the ocean.
Everything I know is this locked ward and constant circling above.
Sometimes I see a plane when the aide takes us to dinner
through the padlocked courtyard to the cafeteria, or a glimpse

of impossibly green grass. When dinner's done, it's too late
to view once-in-this-lifetime meteor showers.

Say anything in Trauma Group. Name your secret: *fathers, brothers,
kindly neighbors, your fourth grade teacher, your mother.* How it happens
over and over. Here's the place for words no one outside wants to hear,
though you've been trying to speak for years.

When the real Beverly shows up to take the old man home to Akron, I
    stare.
Nervous, her head is a helmet of nut-brown hair. She flutters
around the nurses' station. *How can you take him back?* I'm not allowed
to ask. We're protected from him by ten-foot invisible boundaries.

> *Do you see us old man, how we tremble
> out of nightmares weeping? Do you wish now
> you hadn't touched them? Do you look
> at the circle of chairs?*

On his last day, he presses a small gift into everyone's palm
but mine. *Look,* Sarah says, *see what James made?* Tiny origami purses,
construction of sharp paper and careful angles. *It's for mad money.*
Charmed, Sarah barely touches a finger to its center. It gapes open.

Remember this, Lucy says. *Truth forever climbs out of your head,
itchy bump, bug bite gone mad. Trust her.
She keeps us safe.*

DRUNK

What's the drunkest you've ever been,
he's asking. *Tell me.*
As if I've forgotten the perfect stillness
when my head fills with a luscious
rising, each new drink a pink
orbit around my head. I swallow it all.
Blackouts, I say, remembering
what it's like to step so far outside
that the body still continues. *Once
I drank a fifth of whiskey on a bet.* Eighteen
and aching, almost a rock
and roll death, a tangle of dried vomit
in my hair. I woke up. *A man
gave me a gun in a bar,* and I sat on it, hiding
the metal lump under the thick spread
of my thighs. It pinched. *I left eggs
boiling on the stove,* wandered home hours later
to their lovely, moist explosions,
all the water fizzed away. Vanished. Their hard
little shells, dead white scraps littering
the kitchen counters. *Had sex with a stranger
at a party.* I left him there, on the shower stall floor
when it was over, unconscious and dribbling
into the drain. *Stole three thousand cocktail swords
from a bar's closet,* my coat pocket stuffed
with their unsettled sharpness, then I tossed them
in someone's yard. *I threw up
on a woman's shoe.* My lover's mother didn't seem
surprised. She washed her foot, mopped
the floor and my pale face, put me back to bed.
Drunk enough to meet you,
I tell him, remembering our walk home
through the woods, staggering over snow

packed hard enough to hold us up.
We roll over in the cold dark, dizzy,
dizzy with what? *Drunk enough for you,* I say.

NEVER CONSTRUCT NARRATIVE

1.
Huge shadow erection, an inflatable balloon
stolen from a bizarre parade,

sort of like the blow-up doll
we discovered in an unused room

at my daughter's school, pile of porn
magazines, someone's hiding place.

Only this is on the ceiling. Look away,
count to twenty. It's still there.

2.
I'm thirteen again, brand new babysitter.
One child adores me as I sit on the floor
and play dolls. The eighteen-month-old

runs, though when it's time to change
her diaper, she allows me to lift her
to the table, unpin the soaking cloth.

And it's true, thirty years later,
in this mix of vulnerability and business-
as-usual, I'm thinking *How easy*

to harm a child, and no one
would ever know.

3.
Streaky smoke from a thousand packs of cigarettes,
my childhood's familiar fragrance,
overwhelming. I smell it when I make
my grandmother's date-nut pudding,

my father's favorite, on Christmas Eve,
in my therapist's office. Curious times.
Do you smell cigarettes? I ask my daughter

in line at the grocery store. *Mom,
no one's smoking here,* she says in a patient voice
I'm beginning to dislike. *There's
no one smoking at all.*

4.
My father's final words were
a song: *Good Night Ladies.*

Then he died. Tonight
at the movies, I hear him singing

beside me, but I don't bother to turn
while he sings *Many brave hearts*

*are asleep in the deep,
so beware,* still trying
for the low note.

5.
*Do you want to know why
it's an error to create narrative,*

the shrink asks. Please explain
the memories, odors, enormous shadow cock

I see on the ceiling. *Your mind
reveals a glimpse of what's*

too painful to remember more fully.
How can the door knob rattle

and twist when no one is there?
All you get are scraps. Don't string

them into a story. Just take them
as they come. Like when I see my dead father

standing behind me, barely out
of the corner of my eye? *Accept them*

as they reveal themselves. They
come from so far away. Lemons

from the tree in the front yard,
chopped into wedges, so sour

I squirm in yellow waves
of juice. It's everywhere and

it stains as it stings. *You must*
accept them. Oh, I promise, I will.

THE TENANTS

I saw them everywhere: in the backyard
spiraling up inside the pale lilacs, invisible

in the hall closet where old books were stored,
even playing in the fireplace ash. Late at night,

I'd bump into them in the bathroom. The tile floor
was icy and they were on their knees, all those

homeless spirits, blowing night air into a cold fog.
They watched me learn to dance over that floor,

my feet turning blue as a fresh bruise. Oh, they
were in the basement too, snoozing and snoring,

exhaling clouds of oil fumes and dirt from every duct.
Mostly, I heard them laugh. Very late, after everyone was in bed,

they sailed into my room, telling me *Roll over.*
But they were restless, climbing out the window

and ruining the ivy if I so much as blinked twice.
Leave, I'd say, but they'd look limp and listless, even

a bit damp and I'd say *Never mind.* They were most comfortable
in candlelight, safe in the dining room where my mother

set places for them each night when the dark outside
matched the darkness inside. She created a feast

of letters and numbers, the words *yes* and *no.*
How they loved to sip from the highball glass she tilted

upside down, how they hurried to fill up that glass! We watched
their giddy spins over the tabletop forming chains of letters

and words. My mother asked them so many questions,
like *Why not move in?* Little droplets shivered over the table

and they lapped it all up. Once invited, they never left.
They kept me up all night with silent chatter, like visiting

children who don't know when *Dinner in five minutes*
really means *Go home.* They thrust tiny fingers

down the neck of my pajamas, accused me of hogging
the covers, spoke all night of *Secret messages.*

Bored, they stooped to stealing car keys then
cash, gossiping about our careless fumblings,

never minding that I was listening,
that I heard it all.

THIS COLLAPSING WORLD

—for my mother

1.
I hate his touch, my mother tells me. The moon outside stays outside,
small shivers of light. In this dark place, this nursing home,

at night, it's quiet after meds and bed baths. Sometimes the window's
nothing but sky. Two old women roommates, sleeping
And I am awake, she says. His hands, nighttime aide, are working hands,

such rough skin. *I cannot move, haven't moved* from hospital beds
and wheelchairs for years. *I do not want him,* she says. It's not every

night, but listen. How to save us? This cold room he likes
best, *Iced breath in my ear, touching when I cannot speak.*
His shoes soundless beside the bed. *How long, please,*

I'm asking. Send me to another place.

2.
How does the body stiffen, each joint and corner?
It's flat little puddles where water beads,
my mother's hands slipping. Oh, of the body, by the body,

is her body filling with some strange light? All
her fingers are lank petals and inside is rose, redness,

dark passion. It's not easy, this pain she cannot
contain. How many times was she told to be perfect,
to be still. This bowl holds warm water and her hand

is a cup longing to be open again. She says she
understands but to never move again! When this touching

is over, the caretakers, women in white, don't understand her, just wrap her in warm sleep. She counts and counts. It's either left or right and even this body—well, it's enough.

THERAPY-INTERFERING BEHAVIOR

Roxy's cheeking nighttime meds,
right in front of the nurses
who make us stand at the counter
washing pills down
one at a time. Roxy swaps *ambien*

for five bucks and a *percoset*
with another patient. *Is that
a good deal?* I ask. I get two,
and never once thought
to spit them out and make a little money.

I'd rather sleep. When I got here, the nurses
searched my body and my suitcase, confiscated
chapstick because *Medicated*
was on the label. It took a doctor's order
to get it back from the contraband room.

For two nights, Nicole was a patient.
It's the hospital or jail, she said,
but didn't explain. Then she ate
all our snacks: twenty-five packets
of cookies. Bingeing and purging.

She blamed staff for not stopping
her. *That's therapy-interfering behavior,*
Libby told us in a special group meeting.
They kicked Nicole out, so I guess
she's in jail. On Sundays

my husband brings a hot dog with extra onions,
and tomatoes. He has to unwrap
it at the counter before I get it.

At night, the unit shuts down
like a dying daisy, the nurses'

station's surrounded by mattresses stripped
from their beds. They look a little like broken petals.
Those on high suicide watch
or active self-harmers have to sleep here,
twenty-four hour direct observation.

A couple of nights ago my new roommate
tore her bandaged wrists while sleeping,
reopened the wounds. Her spattering blood
drenched the bed linens. Now I have the room
to myself. I say *I'm sorry* to her but I'm not.

Every morning I still wake at four,
take a little stroll down the hall. Someone's
sitting in the safe chair, coloring,
a couple of patients are sobbing.
A few manage to sleep somehow,

their stuffed toys lost in rumpled blankets,
their arms flung out,
curled on plastic mattresses
under the constant light.

THE AFTERNOON MY MOTHER WEARS A PILLOWCASE OVER HER HEAD

to protect her ten dollar wash
and set from bird droppings makes
me sorry, somehow, for the cat
who brought the bird into the apartment.
The pillowcase is satin, slightly askew,
a pink pale as the deep interior
of her cat's narrow throat. I've
come today with a dozen oranges,
their ripeness familiar bumps inside
the paper sack. Mother's sitting
in the green recliner, a cigarette
burning down to ash in her good right hand.
That idiot cat, she says, her voice
muffled under the cloth. I drop the fruit.
Oranges spin to the balcony's half-open
door. The cat waits on the threshold.
My mother's cut holes in the case but they don't
match her eyes. How did she light
that cigarette? Her bad arm's useless,
knitted to her waist. The bird must be small,
stupid from the quick catch. Shredded
feathers blend into cat fur, their
trapped hearts thumping. Ash falls,
silver sparks radiant on the floor. I still
can't see her face, just the wild tears
in soft cloth. It started to fly then,
up to each corner of the room. Completely
quiet, hard, brushing walls, bruising
the ceiling. I saw it catch a breath,
then it flew some more. She won't
take the pillowcase off, no matter how many
times I ask. I'm looking for the bird
in this small apartment. It isn't here.

MY BOYFRIEND'S A VAMPIRE

My boyfriend's a vampire, the first job candidate says,
fingering each red explosion scalloping her neck. Literally
dozens of hickeys. Interviewing's new to me. She wants

to take care of my mother. What's the correct response?
It's all he can get, she says, unbuttons her blouse to reveal
a necklace of stinging *oh's* spooling down to her bra.

He's in prison, she adds, as if that settles it. Then the ambulance
pulls up, bringing my mother from the nursing home. Now she requires
24 hour care. *I can start work now,* she says, knows I don't have a choice.
Surely she's harmless, but when my mother says *I want to meet*

the boyfriend, I have to think it over. *What does this woman want?*
I mean prison's been a movie backdrop or our hometown two cell jail
I visited one Girl Scout field trip. Locked up for a minute was enough,

though several girls wanted more. *Is this merely entertainment?*
Just yesterday, I saw on the news some inmate caught on tape
performing a six minute sex act for his blonde attorney.

They didn't see the security camera. Stuck behind glass,
yet his hands were moving. In the morning paper
she says they're in love but he's quoted as *No comment,*

attorney-client privilege. Prison's confinement's a confusion
of love bites, damp hands in crumpled clothing. *Okay, go ahead and
visit,* I tell my mother. Let the home health aide give up her usual

hickeys and the contraband dollar bills slipped into his hand. Now
she wheels my mother past desire, watchful and open-legged.
The state prison's an hour away and the outing will do her good.

HOW HE SAVES ME

—for D.S.

Last summer I spent an entire morning
examining expensive handbags. Reaching
into store shelves, skimming metal skeletons

with their weight of strappy bags, I touched brown, black,
even whimsical straw. Finally I bought one I didn't need
or want. I liked its secret compartment for keys. David,

my therapist, returning dawn's desperation call,
insists I get rid of my pills. I shook my stash from my grandmother's
bone china teapot, dug at the lining of my new purse, bottle

in the nightstand, even those secrets, melting in the darkness
of my closed fist. This morning David asks during therapy *Do you know*
anyone who chose to live? My friend Carolyn bought a gun

at a pawnshop. The first time she fired was into her mouth.
Randy was a simple overdose and Sweetie refused the tumor
until it was too late. My favorite death was Harry's, rock and roll

on the radio, car chugging in the garage as he fell asleep.
I've acquired more pills. Not a lethal dose, mind you,
just-in-case. *Give them up or go back to the hospital,*

David says at our emergency session, marches me
to the psychiatrist's private bathroom. So I toss the pills
into the scrubbed bowl. Notice their bright flare as they scuttle

to the bottom, tumbling little gems? *Flush it,* he says. Dr. K.
says hello as we pass him in the hall. *Do you feel like an alcoholic,*
pouring a bottle into the sink? Such heaviness in my chest,

then David takes the empty bottle and won't give it back. I remember everyone in the hospital, hundreds of brilliant plans. I'm so ordinary, the same-old same-old. *I'm such a failure,* and then I cry.

BLEEDING OUT

is the easiest death, someone told me. The brain
relaxes, everything ticks slow motion,

as the heart's circles pause
and the gathering pool turns wine, thick.

On the doctor's table, leaking sugar and color,
I was willing to drain away. Not all deaths

are this simple. Some hearts refuse to give,
even as noise disappears. My mother couldn't speak,

couldn't say *I'm ready* when the bedside machines
slowed their clatter. I waited, sure as rain,

until her lungs spasmed and she lived
two more evenings. My daughter,

age seven, said *Let her decide when to die*
and maybe it was true. Her eyes open, staring past me

to the foot of the bed, blood's shallows
slow along her body's folds, holding her

to that promise that she will finally die.
Still her chest rose, puffing towards the end.

It wasn't easy, no blood bath curdling sticky
like breast milk or urine's sweet currents.

The body does what it will.

THE SPIRIT BABY

You're not pregnant, the doctor said as his hands
eased from my belly's throbbing lump.
Then he pressed his ear to my stomach, which wiggled
under his weight and all his scratchy hair. The baby
kicked or burped, or rolled over. *No heartbeat,*
he said. How could he miss those nubby elbows
and fluttering knees battering my flesh?
Get dressed. As he talked, I told my imagination
to shut up and be still. *Some women want a baby so much,*
they convince themselves they're expecting,
he said. Just this morning, tiny drops glittered
over my nipples, bright circles gathering. *Therapy's*
what you need, he said, told me to get dressed.
Now, what to tell this pretend child jolting
under my ribs? It swims and grows,
its little heart hammers. *Maybe a blood test will*
convince you. I've heard mothers and babies
share blood, threading through a long leaky tube.
Take that blood. This baby's mad enough to flip over,
push upside down, nod into position, and say
Wait here. I smile, my belly full of rushing water.

MY DAUGHTER NOTICES THE STRANGER

in the neighbor's yard across the street,
crouching, his pants around his ankles,

collapsing into the choppy grass. *What's
he doing*, she asks, and truth is, it's hard to tell.

Off balance, he stands, yanks his shirt
to his neck, clasps hands beneath

his enormous belly, and turns toward the last
of the afternoon. He's all display. *Maybe he's homeless,*

she wonders, while he stutters half-steps, basking beside
the sidewalk. *I was on the street once,* I tell her, and it's nearly true.

Sleeping in wrinkled clothes, dragging a knapsack
and wishing for a bath *I didn't like it much.* Kicked outside

to search for work after a breakfast of oily oatmeal
and earnest hymns, I sat on benches sneering

at passers-by. Never was I so gloriously naked
in the middle of the day, so ecstatic in the luxury

of bone, I needed to share it. He's picking up leaves,
and kissing their tattered paper. Later, when the cop asks

neighbors gathering in my yard, *Who saw his penis?*
I have to say *I did.* A stranger holding himself, his broad stomach

colliding with the last cold light, finding what we've
all been given, stroking his skin, every bit in two giant hands.

ADOLESCENT UNIT

In the expected warren of corridors,
locked doors, and lunatics, I peer
through a lozenge shaped window,
waiting. Twenty-five years ago
when my brother-in-law roamed the VA hospital
in faded pajamas and robe, my husband
called it the nuthouse. Vietnam vets fretted
while starchy hands unlocked the medication cart,
the narrow ward foggy from a thousand
cigarettes. When group therapy's over,
a chalkboard announces daily goals: *Not to hate
my parents; Not to be suicidal; I just want
to go home.* The main goal clearly is
Keep busy so kids in socks sweep the floor
or tinker with puzzles until someone flips a table,
sending tattered pieces flying. *They hate me because
I can keep my laces,* my daughter says, gestures
to her shoes. She doesn't discuss the shallow scars
lashing her body, hides her stuffed bear. *It's contraband*
unless someone cuts off its head. No one
belongs. Kids drift past, herded by someone
with an ID badge. Never brave enough to look,
I don't know if our daughter turns in our direction.
I remember how my husband
used to slip his brother ten bucks for a carton of Luckies,
though he hates smoking. *It gives him something
to do.* I hear their slippers and socks whisper the hallways.
Airy steps, endlessly shushing away.

LAST DAY IN PARIS

Idly watching pilgrims at prayer,
I set out two candles for my dead parents,
let them burn. When I stepped

into the psych hospital, I was afraid.
When I stepped from the cathedral,
beggars swarmed me, women dressed
in bright gauzes, babies on their hips.

American? As I nodded, a woman in violet
stuffed a tattered paper
into my hand. *I require
money.* Surprised, I stepped back

as she screamed *I must have cigarettes.*
She chased me across the river
until I returned her note.
Sometimes we are all beggars.

I recited my medications
to the hospital psychiatrist *zoloft,
seroquel, buspar, lithium,
ambien, tegretol, ristoril, effexor.*

Then added *They took away
the xanax. Jesus,* he said, *that's quite
a list. Let's tinker with the meds.* Every morning
he slid the window open at the nurses'

station and waited for his patients. *We sing:
we want to sleep, we desire nightmares to lift us,
voices to quiet. We are so tired of visions.*
Change dictated by his careful hands,

gentler than any priest. *You want to be well?*
I wanted an evening boat ride down the Seine,
my chance to pretend I was Audrey Hepburn
dressed to the teeth, hollow background

of *Moon River* as I floated along
the best view of city lights. But,
how strange, the river was rising and streets
were flooding. I saw a small white car

wedged in the graceful arch of a bridge
where it floated. I didn't get what I wanted.
Do we always require a little more? *You're
over medicated,* the psychiatrist said and I nodded.

I have a million ideas, he said. So I stayed alive
another four weeks. The morning
I left the hospital he held out a piece of paper
with one word written across it—*Depression.*

It was instead of the truth—*Bi-polar.* He told me,
*You don't know who sees your medical records.
This will protect you.* He pressed the crisp sheet
into my hand, hoping we believed the lie. *The truth*

*means trouble. People don't understand mental illness.
You will be judged, labeled, never get a decent job,* he said,
explaining my future without the paper, without the lie.

WATER LANDING

Not a man I could love, though
I went with him to the picnic
where we ate sweet yellow corn shaved
from the cob and bowls of dripping
fruit. A slice of cantaloupe beamed,
strange and happy, even with
its rim of angry green. He walked me
to the lake in the strange near dark
along a road where we left our clothes
in separate piles. I wish I could say
the warm water raised us into one another,
that this was a man I could hold all the way
to the lake's cloudy center. The chilly
water smelled of dying, of fish, greenness,
slime. Floating face down at the edge,
I walked my hands along the mucky bottom,
liking the strong pull of thick mud, the wrap
of unfamiliar plants on my white skin.
He pushed behind me then, his sharp small
hips striking my flesh, slapping the water
into arches rising above our backs.
Lazy branches bent over the gray
water, and something fine rose through
the trap of smoky summer evening.
I was sinking into old soil, my face wet
with whatever gathered below the surface.
Then he waited on shore while I watched
the wavy surface grow pitted with small
drops. Clothes I hurried into were strangely
binding as I left the water behind, washed
and glistening, strangely undressed.

STUDY IN FLOWERS

I.
Unidentifiable fresh flowers
in a plastic jug on the hospital room desk,
fantastic orange blooms stumbling
into purple, fist of pinks.
My husband selects them

at the outdoor market, gaudiest
colors, to tempt me
with vividness as well as the unfamiliar.
Who wants daisies when you
can look into a face bigger

than a plate, wired to a green stick
to prop its silly head?
I don't know their names, petaled
darlings, California garden
of pure astonishment. He brings

a new bouquet every Sunday,
visiting day, replacement.
Frivolous with their newness, I toss
the old flowers into the garbage can
in my room. Leftovers,

all their color bled away this week
as they worked hard not to bend,
not to shiver in the cool hospital air.
Finally overcome, graceful,
beyond full bloom.

2.
Plenty of light and water
along with good soil is necessary
for a perfect plant. My father's

simple recipe, repeated
each time I slip into the greenhouse.
He coils the hose around

his trunk, showers beds
of chrysanthemums. As a child
I loved to watch their tight

palms unfurl, sprays of petals
like ballerina ruffles upside
down. Some early Saturdays

we drove downtown
to the wholesale house to sell entire
truckloads. *Remember the push*

and muscle, bronzes, lavenders,
gold and white, how they shoved
their heady way through the open doors?

3.
Your flowers smell so good
they stop me in the hallway.

The nurse slips in, touches
her face to the bunched centers.

How odd, I didn't notice
any fragrance, though I dutifully

bend and inhale. I nod, friendly
gesture, don't tell her I smell

emptiness, and loss. Patients
admire them too, remark

on their heavy scent, how it fills
my room and the entire hall.

NOVEMBER

This sudden sweep
of wings most unlikely,
seven ordinary birds

rushing the narrow corridor.
They fly towards the locked door
where they bank and turn,

a lovely arch in this stillness.
One breath lifting past
our rooms, down to the dayroom,

beyond the soda machine.
One more spin. We stand
and watch this exhalation,

outdoors strangely indoors.
During the final trip
one small bird loses its way,

plows through the nurses' station,
stops dead in the staff room.
The others leave it behind, of course,

aim for the open door, no doubt
headed for the Pacific Ocean's
scented wind just blocks away.

We're stunned. Does
survival arrive uninvited,
and what about the lost bird?

No wild wing beats, no
noise. A patient shoulders
her way in, and between

her cupped hands I glimpse
one bitter eye.
She walks to the patio,

half a ruined tennis court
surrounded by a locked
fence, grassless, without

flowers. She sets the bird
on cement. It hops
a few times before

it finally unruffles
its wings and lifts directly
into the damp air.

A Note on the Author

Virginia Chase Sutton comes from a family of women writers. Her great-aunt, Mary Ellen Chase, was a well-known author of fiction and non-fiction in the mid-twentieth century. Her grandmother, Virginia Lowell Chase, published two novels and a collection of essays. Sutton holds an MFA from Vermont College and is a former English professor. Her poems have appeared in *The Paris Review*, *Ploughshares*, *The Antioch Review*, *Western Humanities Review*, and *Quarterly West*, among others. Her first book of poems, *Embellishments*, was published by Chatoyant in 2003. Sutton was born and raised in the Midwest, and lives in Tempe, Arizona, with her husband and daughters.

A Note on the Prize

The Samuel French Morse Poetry Prize was established in 1983 by the Northeastern University Department of English in order to honor Professor Morse's distinguished career as teacher, scholar, and poet. The members of the prize committee are: Francis C. Blessington, Joseph deRoche, Victor Howes, David Kellogg, Ellen Noonan, Stuart Peterfreund, and Guy Rotella.

Library of Congress Cataloging-in-Publication Data

Sutton, Virginia Chase.
  What brings you to Del Amo / Virginia Chase Sutton ; selected and introduced by Charles Harper Webb.
      p. cm. — (Morse poetry prize)
  ISBN-13: 978–1–55553–689–3 (pbk. : alk. paper)
  ISBN-10: 1–55553–689–1 (pbk. : alk. paper)
  I. Webb, Charles Harper. II. Title.
  PS3619.U896W47 2007
  811'.6—dc22   2007018187